?OHODI GHĄ DOLNI

Diri eritł'is sekui honeltën kóę t'a?u nįdárodi ghą honį

TELLING the TRUTH

A Story-telling Activity on the Residential School Experience

PAGC Taghë Ts'en Eritł'is Dene Ts'enį

ʔOHODI GHĄ DOLNI

Diri eritł'is sekui honeltën kóę t'aʔu nįdárodi ghą honį

Residential School Stories – Sekui Honeltën Kóę ts'į Honį

TELLING the TRUTH

A Story-telling Activity on the Residential School Experience

Edward Mirasty and Vince Brittain
Translation by Rosalie Tsannie-Burseth

Copyright 2023 Prince Albert Grand Council. All rights reserved.

Published by:
Big Moose Publishing
Box 127 Site 601 RR#6
Saskatoon, SK S7K 3J9
www.bigmoosepublishing.com

ISBN: 978-1-989840-60-3
Big Moose Publishing 06/2023

TABLE of CONTENTS

Mission Statement	7
Book Cover Artist	8
Telling the Truth	9
Importance of the Circle	10
Importance of Sharing their Stories	11
Acknowledgements	12
Seven Grandfather Teachings	15
Gordon Behonié/Gordon's Story	17
George Behonié/George's Story	29
Information on Residential Schools	38
Biographies	39
About the Authors	40
Participant's Comments	42
Help Line for Residential School Survivors	43
Bibliography	44

MISSION STATEMENT

The Prince Albert Grand Council Executive will provide leadership in a comprehensive way to address issues of common concern that affect PAGC First Nation communities and its members, including Treaty protection, resource development and revenue sharing.

(PAGC Chief's Strategic Plan, 2021, p. 3).

Grand Chief Brian Hardlotte, member of Lac La Ronge Indian Band, was elected in October 2017 and is serving his 2nd term as Grand Chief.

Vice Chief Joseph Tsannie, member of the Hatchet Lake Denesuline First Nation; was re-elected in October 2015 and is serving his 3rd term as Vice Chief.

Vice Chief Christopher Jobb, member of Peter Ballantyne Cree Nation; was elected in October 2016 and is serving his 2nd term as Vice Chief.

BOOK COVER ARTIST

Dennae is part Cree and Dené and is a thirteen-year-old urban Indigenous artist who loves art. Art is one of her favorite subjects in school. Dennae's background includes her family such as her mom who is Cree, her dad is Dené and her big brother is part Cree and Salteaux-Ojibwe. Dennae has enjoyed art as a hobby ever since she could hold a crayon. She would spend her fun time at the table coloring, drawing and that continued with doodling on her work at school. Wherever she saw space she created an art piece even if it was tiny, she let her imagination of art grow. Dennae has won in art competitions in her school which includes a buffalo piece that was purchased by Vincent Massey School for the school year of 2021-22.

It is hanging in the school hallway for all to see. Her art pieces also include a crane "Endangered Animals" category that was part of a class project. The crane art piece was selected to compete in the Saskatchewan Rivers art contest. Dennae's crane art piece won the award of excellence winner for 2022 in the Grade 7 to 9 category. Her current art piece of the "215+ Indigenous Reconciliation" is a tribute to the murdered and missing children who never made it home and for those who did make it home. Dennae is still attending Christina's Art school for at least 5-6 years. She enjoys art styles such as acrylic, graphite and oil pastels. Art is her passion and enjoys telling stories through her artwork. Dennae is an author, co-author and illustrator for the book she wrote with her mom called "Dennae's Angel Star" for little and big people on loss and grieving. You must read both books to understand the loss from a child's heart to a mom's heart. Support Indigenous youth such as Dennae who enjoys pursuing her gifts such as art and writing.

TELLING the TRUTH

As part of the Prince Albert Grand Council and Saskatchewan Polytechnic's initiative, an important event has taken place in response to the Truth and Reconciliation's Calls to Action.

A one-day storytelling session took place at the Hannin Creek Facility next to Candle Lake, Saskatchewan. The activity called "Telling the Truth," shares the lived experiences of two former Indian Residential School Survivors.

IMPORTANCE of the CIRCLE

"Talking circles are a traditional indigenous method of information sharing and decision making used by a group to discuss a topic in an egalitarian and non-confrontational manner."
(Fleischhacker et al. 2011; Brandenburger et al. 2016)

IMPORTANCE of SHARING THEIR STORIES

Sharing the history of the trauma experienced by Indigenous Peoples is imperative in creating children's storybooks. For instance, Peterson & Robinson (2020) note, "they need to be shared through intergenerational storytelling and picture books created by Indigenous authors who have firsthand experience or pass down stories from their parents and grandparents," (p. 6)

This sharing can lead to better understanding, on the part of Indigenous and non-Indigenous children, of the intergenerational impact of these horrific assimilative practices.

ACKNOWLEDGEMENTS

The Prince Albert Grand Council would like to thank Saskatchewan Polytechnic for allowing the use of their facility in Hannin Creek. The PAGC Executive and staff also thank the two elders, Gordon and George, from PAGC Holistic Health, for sharing their stories.

Finally, this book would not have been possible for the leadership of Grand Chief, Brian Hardlotte.

Shortly after arrival, people walked towards the Hannin Creek campgrounds, while others sat around the crackling fire pit.

After everyone arrived, participants gathered inside the octagon-shaped building to grab one of twenty chairs placed in a circle.

SEVEN GRANDFATHER TEACHINGS

George Mirasty

Gordon Keewatin

In their analysis of Indigenous story-telling, Peterson & Robinson (2020) share the importance of integrating cultural norms through, "The Seven Grandfather Teachings: wisdom, love, respect, bravery, honesty, humility, and truth [42], the teachings explain roles and responsibilities at each part of the life circle," (p. 8).

Having the story-telling session take place in the outdoors (Hannin Creek facility) allowed participants to gather and listen to the stories shared by the two Elders.

To begin the story-telling experience in a good way, one of the elders started with a **smudge ceremony**.

GORDON BEHONIÉ

GORDON'S STORY

Sekui hesłį-u, dįghį sëghayé hots'į Ɂįłaghëts'atheł hots'ën, setikui bet'azi hiya nį, Deneziyaghë ëya kóę ts'ën (For San). Eyi t'a Deneziyaghë ëya kóę si Fort Qu'appelle hots'į yatthe ts'en hoɁa si naithër ni.

From the age 4 to 11 years of age, I would have to say goodbye to my family beginning with a place called Fort Sand, North Fort Qu' Appelle.

Diri Fort San Dene k'onį si t'a dada bets'į si nokodi-u tth'i hetį hoʔąnelt'e. Kuli t'ąhą t'a-u sëba ëyaile de, yisi Etthié Kóę ełts'ën nibanësa nį. Kuli hok'ëtł'asi hites ʔanohilthënį.

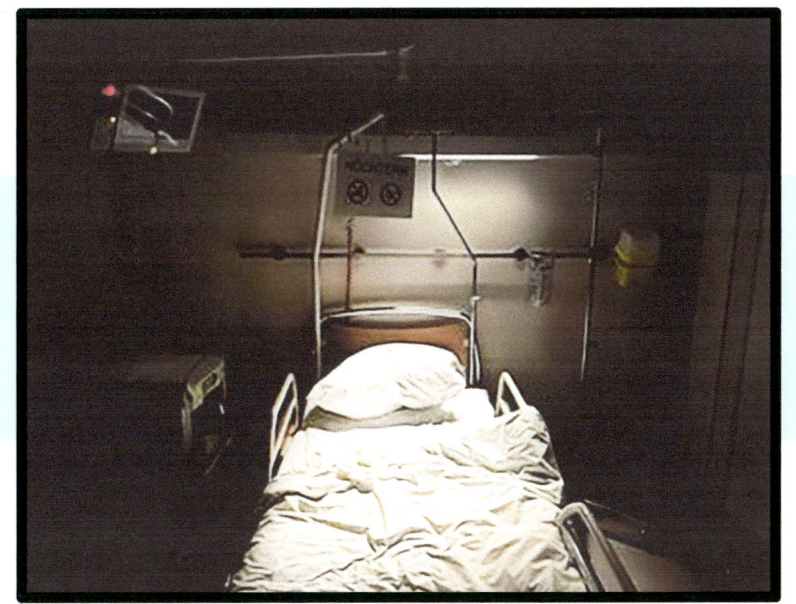

Fort San was a place of rest and recovery from tuberculosis. It was a place where I felt energetic enough to run up and down the halls. We were also forced to stay in bed to keep rested.

Deneziyaghë Kóę hots'į Saskatoon sënënę nat'adh nį. Seth'ene hots'į yazi tth'en hilchu t'a sënënę sëlya ni. Jłaghë nęnę hots'ën ëyër hitį nį, ëyër hots'į Fort San ts'ën nasałtį nį.

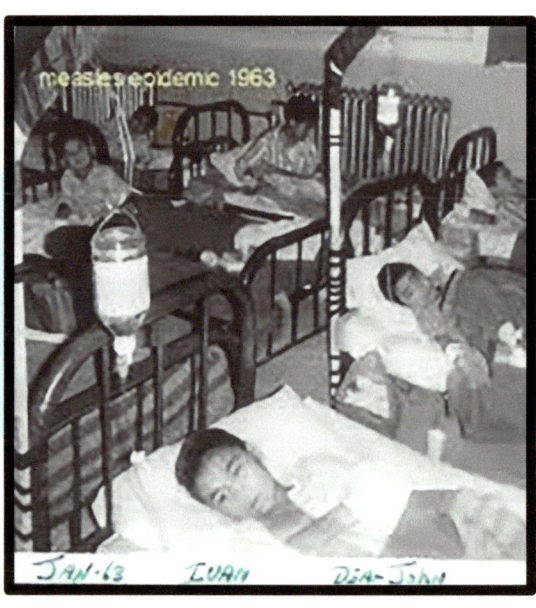
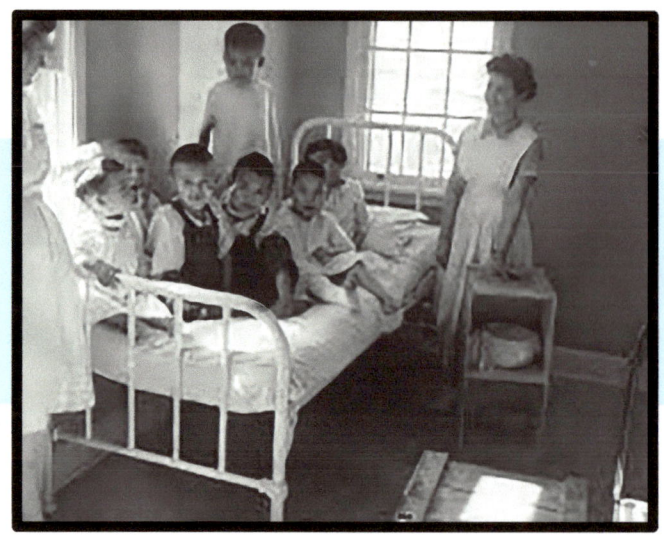

During this time I was shipped to Saskatoon to have an operation on my back. There was a bone graft done and inserted into my spine. I was there for a year and eventually made my way back to Fort San.

Fort San hots'į seredi-u sënëné ts'en thile ts'en nahhësja nį. Ëyër hots'į Sekui Honiltën Kóę sekui k'onį nįsįltį Portage La Prairie, Manitoba ts'ën. Ëyër tthile ts'en naithër nį. Hotł'ąghë Birtle, Manitoba ts'en nįsįltį nį.

Once I was released from Fort San, I returned home only for a short period. I was taken to a Residential School in Portage La Prairie, Manitoba where I stayed for a bit. I would later be sent to Birtle, Manitoba.

Diri Birtle Sekui honełtën Kóę ts'en seheltį nadłį eyit'a nah sekóę t'azi hiya nį.

Birtle Indian Residential School was my second experience leaving home.

Sekui honełtën kóę si, hok'ëtł'azi ełk'įnį nadáriłya ʔanohilthënį. Dzįdónelt'u dayailti lįnį. K'oildele, t'a nuhéts'edi si hiłts'i hoʔa. Diri t'a sekui honełtën kóę si ełelt'e ni. T'aʔu tot'įnë k'ezi daída ʔanohilthënį lįnį.

While in these institutions, we were lined up had to say our daily prayers and we were forced to follow. This happened in both places as a way to assimilate us.

Diri nuneshe ghą náide lįnį. Dzįdónelt'u ëjërë-u, gugus-u, tot'įnë ts'į dih ghąnilchu ghą náide lįnį.

We were forced to work in the garden and on the farm. Most activities included feeding cattle, pigs and chickens on a daily basis.

Bër nuhk'onel?ą ljnį, eyi t'a nuneshe danit'į. Labada nailchi-u nuyaghë tsąthël k'e dáilt'edh ljnį.

Meals were not filling at all and we had to sneak food from the garden. For example, we would take potatoes from the garden and cook them in the basement on the furnace.

T'ąt'u nųhk'onį si horelyįle t'a tsąke-ú, dzoł xal-u, dzoł jiret'ith t'a senaide lįnį.

As a form of escape, we would join sports, such as, hockey, baseball, and soccer.

Tsąke t'a senaide ghądanįdhën lįnį.

Playing hockey was something I loved to do.

Ku eyer hots'į ëritl'is t'a asi herësłër ghąnithį ni.

Eventually, I fell in love with art.

GEORGE BEHONIÉ

GEORGE'S STORY

Jłk'etaghë sëghayé-u Sekui Honeltën Kóę nįsįltį nį Prince Albert, Saskatchewan ts'ën. Ëyër 1960 hots'į 1969 ts'ën naithër nį. Sekui łą bëhchënë yelya-u naltsi nį, nųhhetikui bets'azi nuhhëłya nį. Sechele chu, sedezë chu bëhchënë yenųhhelya nį.

At the age of 6 years of age, I was taken to a Residential School in Prince Albert, Saskatchewan. I stayed there from 1960 to 1969. Like many other children, I was placed in a car with my brothers and sisters only to be taken away from our parents.

Nų heyatié t'a dayailti de nuhhëldhath lįnį, thëdhë cho t'a. T'ahąde ejietthëdh t'a nuhhëldël lįnį.

If we were caught speaking our language we were strapped and grounded. A conveyer-type strap was used for disciplining. Sometimes, they would use a rubber hose.

Sekui honełtën kóę t'a ts'en sekui k'onį si thënë sekui honełtën kóę ts'ën nųhhelye ni. Eyer de t'a tot'įnë k'ezi hadanųhënëltën.

During my time at the Residential School, we transitioned to the town school. This wasn't easy, because we had to learn the colonizer's language.

Sekui honełtën kóę náide nųhhetikui kuli dait'įle nį.

Although we attended the same school, we weren't allowed to visit with our own family members.

Holą Benasni, sëba horelyįle lįnį.

I remember this was a lonely time for us.

T'ąt'u nųhhįnié si įghą beneridi lįnį t'a sekui honełtën nųhk'onį si. Tsąke-u, dzoł xal-u, dzoł ełk'ëch'a yailyuł t'a senaide lįnį.

A person realized very quickly that you had to be good in sports to get away from that lonely feeling. Residential School by playing hockey, baseball, basketball, volleyball etc.

Hotié nëhhodi-u, Dzįdónelt'u dayailti-u, daidzën ʔanohilthënį.

Time was spent in routines that were very rigid like saying daily prayers and singing Christian songs.

Holą bër basthi lįnį, gah ghą bił nesle nį, eyi t'aiłdų asiride lįnį.

Many times I was hungry. We would set up rabbit snares in the nearby bush. This is how we would supplement our meals as we were still hungry.

INFORMATION on RESIDENTIAL SCHOOLS

https://nctr.ca/education/teaching-resources/residential-school-history/

https://fncaringsociety.com/welcome

https://www.edonline.sk.ca/webapps/blackboard/content/listContent.jsp?course_id=_3514_1&content_id=_126393_1&mode=view

https://www.edonline.sk.ca/webapps/blackboard/content/listContent.jsp?course_id=_3514_1&content_id=_300268_1&mode=reset

https://www.thecanadianencyclopedia.ca/en/article/residential-schools

BIOGRAPHIES

Gordon Keewatin

My name is Gordon Keewatin and I am originally from Peepeekeesis First Nation and now I am a member of the Montreal Lake Cree Nation. I am happily married and going on my 50th Anniversary. I have three children and numerous grandchildren. I currently work for the Prince Albert Grand Council. In this role, I work with Indian Residential Survivors, 60s scoop, Indian Day School, and Day Scholars. Also, I am a cultural (Elder) support worker which I enjoy doing.

George Mirasty

My name is George Mirasty from the Lac la Ronge Indian Band. I am happily married and have five children. I am currently employed with the Prince Albert Grand Council. I reside on the Little Red River First Nation. In my current position, I currently work with Indian Residential Survivors, 60s scoop, Indian Day School, and Day Scholars.

ABOUT the AUTHORS

Edward Mirasty

Edward Mirasty is a Cree member of the Lac LaRonge Indian Band and has worked at the Prince Albert Grand Council as Director of Education for over thirteen years, including fourteen years in education. He is happily married for over thirty years to his high school sweetheart, and they both have a little girl named Lilly B. He graduated from the Indian Teacher Education Program (ITEP) in 1994, completed his Master of Education in 2006 (Education Administration), and is currently in his sixth year of a Doctorate of Education through Wilkes University. He is currently a Board of Governor for the First Nations University and has sat at various provincial and national tables including the AFN, FSIN and Provincial Task Teams. Edward loves being outdoors where he can hunt, fish, golf and camp with his family.

Vince Brittain is a James Smith Cree Nation Band member who grew up and attended school at Bernard Constant Community School. He has been married to his wife Connie for over twenty-one years. They have two boys. The eldest, Merit, has completed his second year at the University of Regina in Social Work, and has now entered his first year of Education through the First Nations University of Canada. His youngest, Merik, is attending Grade 12 at Carlton Comprehensive High School. Vince has been involved in education for over 26 years and is currently finishing up his first year of a Doctorate of Education through the University of Saskatchewan. He currently works at the Prince Albert Grand Council as their Third Level Specialist. He believes in honesty, integrity, and trustworthiness, which leads to strong relationships. Vince's parents truly believed in education and strongly supported him in his educational journey. They would be proud of him as he continues with his educational journey and helps empower communities as they move forward.

Vince Brittain

PARTICIPANT'S COMMENTS

"I can't imagine having my four-year grandson being taken away from me at that age." – *Hannin Creek participant, 2021*

"In my seven years being in Canada, I have learned more about Canada's history in one day being here." – *Israel Saskatchewan Polytechnic student, 2021*

HELP LINE FOR RESIDENTIAL SCHOOL SURVIVORS

Indian Residential School Survivors and Family

1-800-721-0066

The Indian Residential Schools Crisis Line is available 24-hours a day for anyone experiencing pain or distress as a result of his or her Residential school experience.

BIBLIOGRAPHY

Peterson, S. S., Robinson, R. B. (2020). Rights of Indigenous Children: Reading Children's Literature through an Indigenous Knowledge Lens. Education sciences. Volume 10 (21). pp. 1-16.

Girl in photo: Lilly B Mirasty

Indigenizing is "emphasizing holistic education over compartmentalized subjects, engaging talking circles, and using traditional arts, crafts, activities, and land-based learning to explore curriculum.[1]"

[1] Morcom, L., Freeman, K. (2018). Niinwi - kiinwa - kiinwi: Building non-indigenous allies in education through indigenous pedagogy. Canadian Society for the Study of Education: Canadian Journal of Education; 41 (3), pp 820

www.ingramcontent.com/pod-product-compliance
Lightning Source LLC
Chambersburg PA
CBHW050847010526
44107CB00017BA/1210